There's A Sponge Growing On My Roof
The Difference a Green Roof Can Make in the World

Roger Grothe
Illustrated by Jeremiah Humphries
Forward by Dr. Susanna Lehvävirta

To Jake, Luke, Jesse, and Lily

There's a Sponge Growing On My Roof
The Difference a Green Roof Can Make in the World

ISBN-13:978-0692025345
Published in 2014

For more information: www.theresaspongegrowingonmyroof.com

There's A Sponge Growing On My Roof
The Difference a Green Roof Can Make in the World

Forward

Dear adult –parent, aunt, grandfather or other VIP – you have a unique book at hand. By sharing this book with children you will show them how the everyday environment can be improved by adding vegetation to it. This is important as most of the people on our planet Earth live in cities and are suffering from floods, heat waves, air pollution, noise and lack of restorative environments. Green roofs are one way to tackle these problems brought about by urbanization.

Green roofs are old – e.g. in Finland they have existed for centuries – but the contemporary solutions are radically different from the old turf roofs. Current green roofs are technical systems that are installed in order to provide a selection of services such as flood control, noise abatement, urban agriculture and enhanced biodiversity. Vegetation has also been scientifically shown to improve people's health and well-being in many ways.

Finland is a small country up in the north, with a long and dark snowy winter, a short but lovely summer and large open wilderness areas. Due to these conditions Finns have a lot of SISU: they are gutsy, persistent – sometimes even stubborn outdoor people. As most Finns nowadays live in cities they are looking for more space, fresh air and nature within the cities. Thus, they are eagerly studying opportunities on the roofs: how could this new space make their lives better? They are experimenting on the roofs of warehouses, saunas, shopping centers, university buildings and blocks of flats. There are meadows, mosses and biodiversity hot spots on the roofs.

Finns are excited about bringing local plants and animals onto roofs. Can wildlife find habitat on the roofs? Will butterflies or other pollinators find their way there? Could the roofs offer habitat for threatened plants? And can the citizens enjoy the beauty of this semi-wild nature? Finns are sure about one thing: it is worth trying. And with a lot of SISU they will build and test all possible kinds of new ideas on the roofs.

Dr. Susanna Lehvävirta
The Fifth Dimension - Green Roofs
Botany Unit - Finnish Museum of Natural History
University of Helsinki

Storms stall

Raindrops fall

Rooftops fill

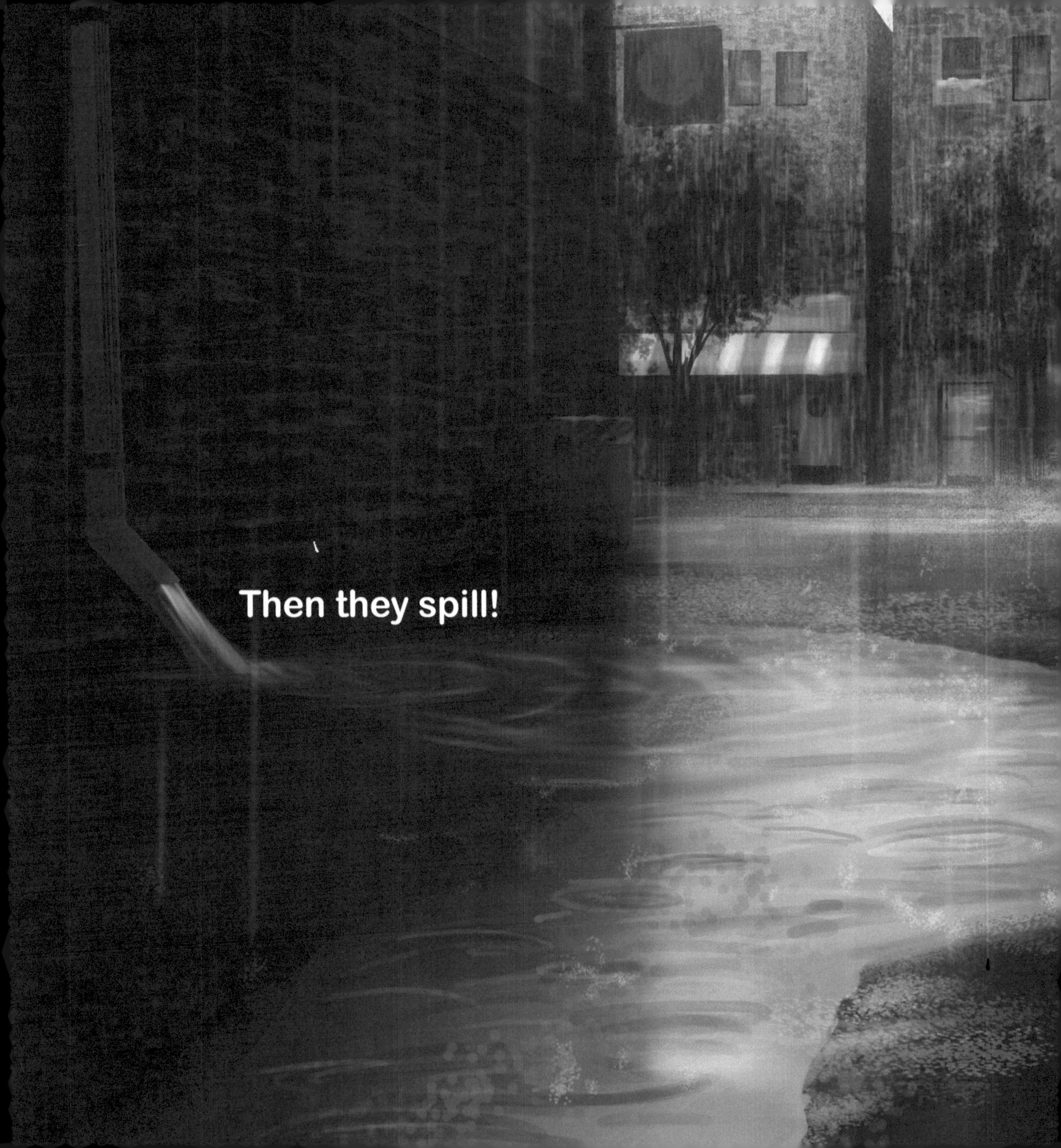

Then they spill!

Faster and faster the water flows

But look, there's no place for
all the water to go

It won't stop soon, no sign
of the sun

Lookout bunnies! Run! Run! Run!

We need more green space
to soak up the rain

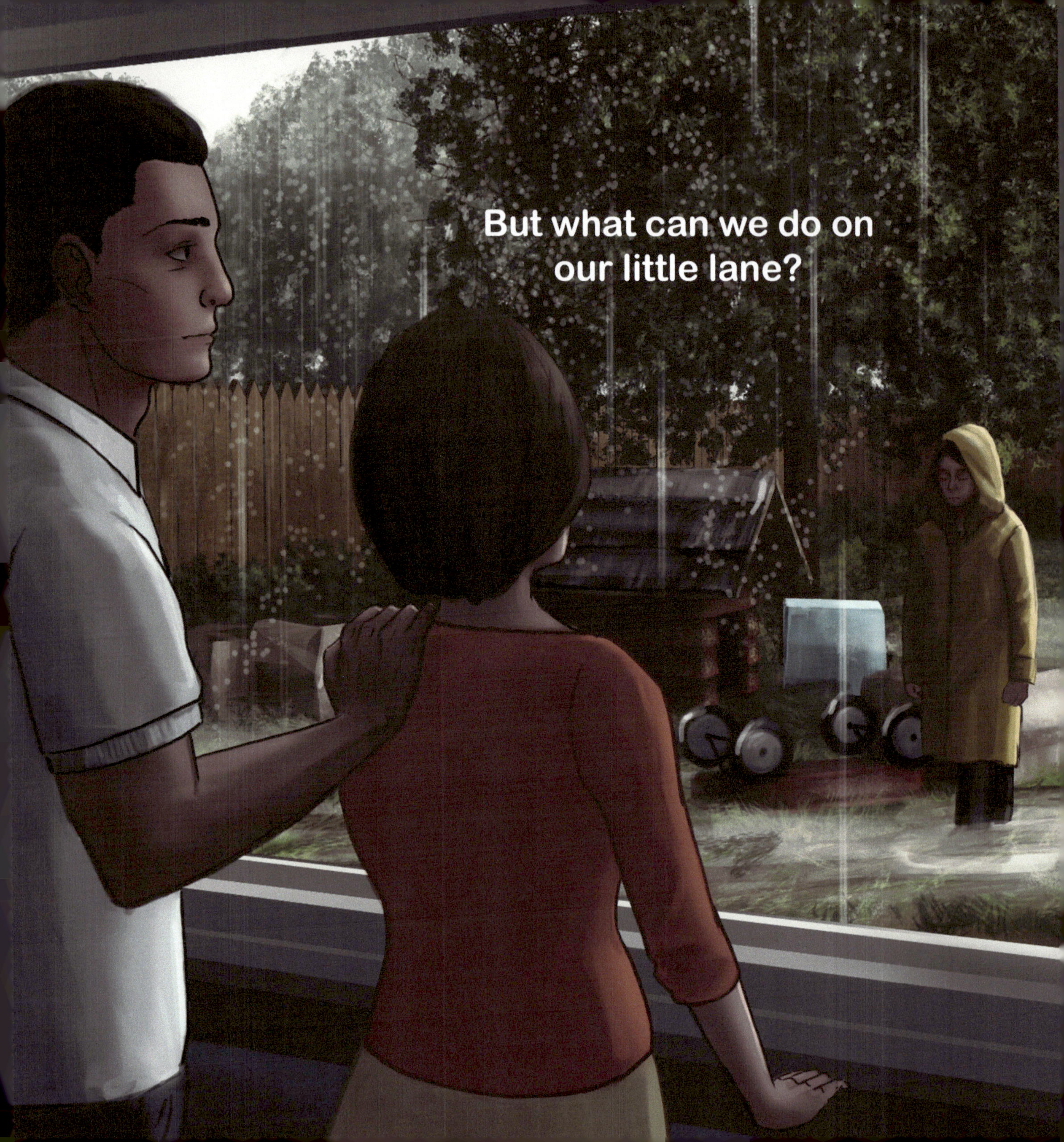

But what can we do on
our little lane?

Parking lots and streets are growing fast

Maybe...

...the answer lies in the past

For hundreds of years green roofs have added green space

Today, green roofs are
all over the place

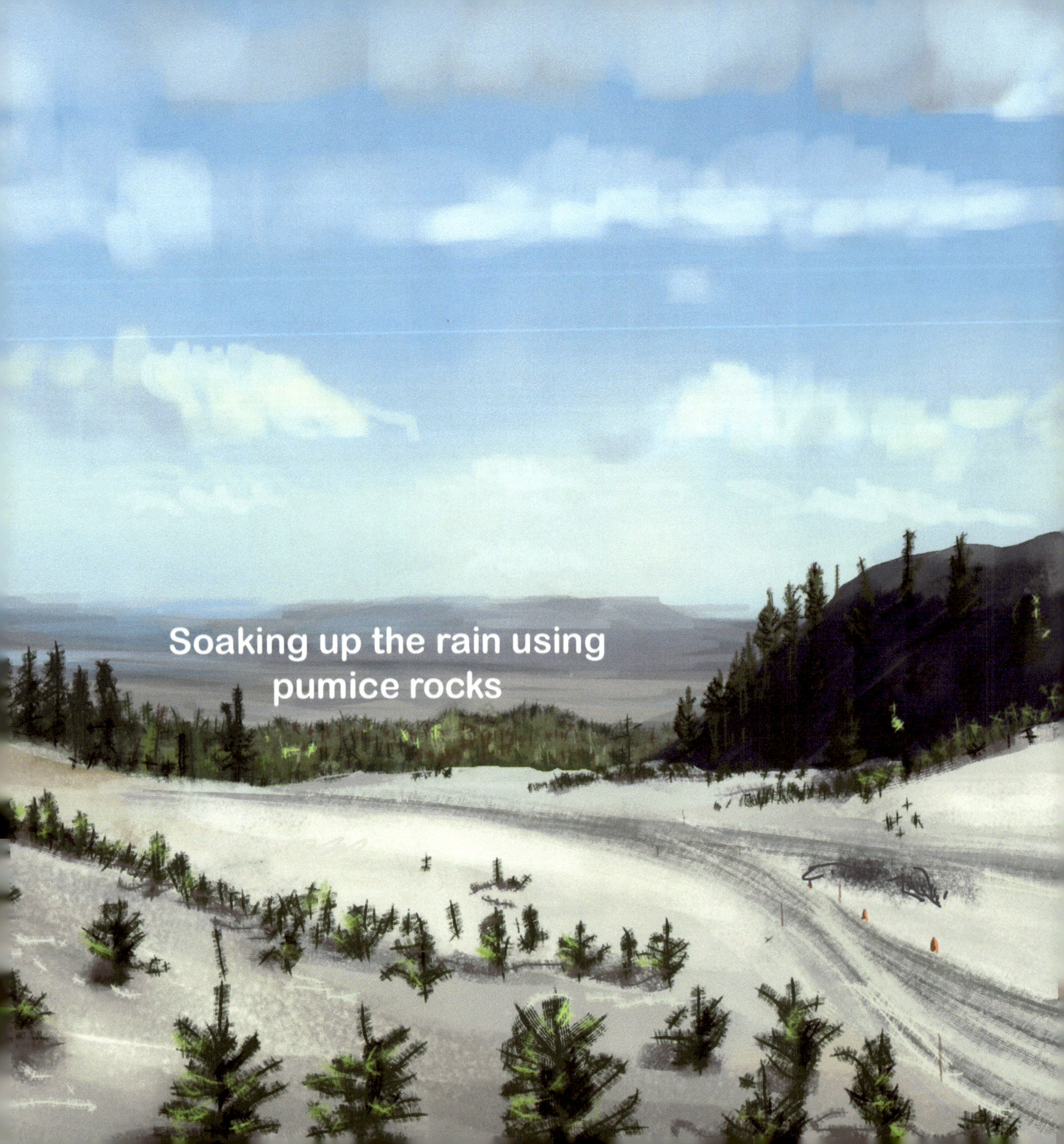

Soaking up the rain using pumice rocks

And releasing it slowly following mother nature's clock

This barren roof we've tried to keep clean

Will be full of life and full of green!

We are building a
green roof

That acts like a sponge

A home for plants, and the
butterflies and bugs

A green space to
catch all the water
that would plunge

Storms stall

Raindrops fall

Our green roof sponge
is catching them all!

Creating new green space
is simple and fun

The end…

... or just the beginning!

www.ingramcontent.com/pod-product-compliance
Lightning Source LLC
Chambersburg PA
CBHW060835270326

41933CB00002B/97